DIRTY SECRET

By Iamgood Chinenye Momah-Eze

"Recovery of Womanhood"

A DIRTY SECRET

ISBN: 978-978-984-371-8

Amazon with Kindle Direct Publishing

Email: iamgoodchinenye@gmail.com

+2347039285655, +234907029310

All scripture quotation is from King James Version Bible.

Let him kiss me with the kisses of his mouth:

for thy love is   better than wine.

I am Black but comely, O ye daughters of Jerusalem,

as the tents of ke-dar, as the

Curtains of Solomon.

Look not upon me, because I am black, because

the sun hath looked upon me: my

Mother's children were angry with me; they made

me the keeper of the vineyards;

But mine own vineyard have I not kept.

I am the rose of Sharon, and the lily of the valleys.

As the lily among thorns, so is my love among the daughters.

He brought me to the banqueting house and

his banner over me was love.

Songs of Solomon: verses from chapter 1 and 2 KJV

Contents

Preface

Do you know the man you married? Is he a king and a Priest? Do you want to take an important step in life like marriage? Then you need to ensure that the man you want to wed is both a King and A priest. Because choice of marriage partner could either make or mar you. Hence marriage is a place of dreams. Where

visions are to be realised not truncated or destroyed.The Book Dirty secrete decodes the nature of a King and Priest. It will tell you a hint on expectation in marriage and what is expected from you as the woman.

It's a must read book. Enjoy as you read.

CHAPTER 1: DRINK WATER FROM HER CISTERN

They didn't tell you that in between those legs lay life, so sweet that you shouldn't let all get a taste of thine pure honey.

They drink water from cisterns you know? ''I rather let a King drink from my own cistern''.

Where them GODS, the GREAT KING and the HIGH PRIEST rule is there the glory is. Where the GOD, the gods, the GREAT KING, the KINGS, THE HIGH PRIEST and PRIEST Rules there the glory will be.When they clad in the attire of Royalty, when they adorn themselves as Priest. Their vestments with the rigour of certainty. They will tell you they earned their title well sought. There is no mistaking. They will shed blood to keep their kingdom. Their ruler ship and kingship will know no end.

I will tell you a tale a King told me, he said women will always be wives and wives will always be brides and brides could earn the title of queens if the people let her but that they kings never give their wives away. They never queen them. Its a title they cherish.

Hence I thought to myself, I did sleep with a King for life and I did wife a King for Life and I thought I had slept with the King for Love.

For woman hood is highly esteemed. Their value added women; at the right hand, the woman is satisfied. They never call her queen.

Wives and Bride is what she is. Their wives will tell you the tale of their Husbands conquer. There are no Queens the women will say. I am a wife and Bride to my King. A queen to find is only earned; the people will tell you she earned the name too well. They say the king agreed he had no option, his people ('s) acceptance meant the most to him, his kingdom is his first priority.

He won't incite a treason hence he knows why he went for a wife and a Bride. He never gives his wife away. His eyes will tell the tale that he knows their queen but he rather keep the status quo of Wife and Bride. He will call her: "The Queen" never my queen. Never do Kings call their wives Queens. They don't share their power, they don't share their Kingship, they don't share their glory but in woman's willingness there her persuasion and influence will be the power to win her King to her side.

"I rather be a wife and Bride; I mean why Queen at all. GOD: Ladies enjoy the tapestry, warm in the upholstery, admire the furniture's, get their seeds to walk in life. Give the help where you are required. I never give my wife away I tell you the truth I never do".

King Husbands Drink water from her cistern and never do mince with words.

Wives tilt your head left, right and speak slightly bow ing thine head it is. Your honour is theirs to find. The King will keep the kingship of his king and preserve the honour of his Royalty. His priesthood will never lack ointment. They will pour clean oil on his head; Fresh from the finest of trees.

Where the GOD, The KINGS AND The HIGH PRIEST is. Thy woman will be well defined. No one can find her womanhood unless GOD the GREAT KING and the HIGH PRIEST is the Head of thy King. That's if a man did ever be king when he fails to let the Great King, The GOD and The High Priest Lead. For Christ is the Head of the Man.

Where the Great King and the high priest is go pour thy expensive ointment at his feet. Let the Oil drip from thy mouth like honey which flows from a honey comb.

Drink water from my cistern only My King and Priest.

CHAPTER 2: GARMENTS ARE FIT FOR A BRIDE

Are you ready to wife the king; it's a high calling that you should never despise.

They tell you that there's traditional fattening room for the Calabars they use it to prepare a woman for marriage. I tell you wife is a life time preparation.

What did you learn in your learning? When to speak, how to speak, where to speak, why to speak and whom to speak to. You want to answer you are married and what did you do to prepare?; I see them women say: they get in relationships and here you are talking about what marriage presents for couples. You waste your time in what does not profit.

Where the Kings ruling is there the glory will be. Get it right; get yourself married and see that the glory will radiate all around you.

You want a dignified life and you spent most of your days at sleep, No chores, No exercises, No plans, No work, No business. O woman, where is the pomegranate given to you. What you don't have will be taken away from you.

They tell you women should put on skirts. You think you know a thing about garments. Go buy your shorts and pants. I did put my Skirts long down to my ankle. I Swag that thing.

You are enclosed and you think it's because you know what it is. Your price is too high that not even a husband will find his way without breaking through your walls.

I wonder why women will give their body to everyone all in the name of some love. A love I know that never exist. True Love is there with GOD, The Great King AND the HIGH Priest.

His Spikenard does send out its smell. There the glory is. His honour is thine to find, There the glory will be.

Where is thy woman? Where are thy Spartan women? Aggressive and prepared for the worst. Not that the worst did ever find any woman by he's word. For if you keep my word happy are you.

Rather: spread your legs with your skirts hang down to the ground. Rather Pack thy hair and Hide within A veil. Don't trade thy womanhood for a temporary pleasure. Really there is no pleasure in 5mins. 20mins will not pleasure. It's a Pleasure for a life time. It is learnt earned and it is of a great gain. It will come with friendship you must agree and it will come with submission that you must accede. Go ask thy Elderly women at the church. The old age widows will tell you that true pleasure lay in the bed for a life time. They will shed their tears. We won't tell you why.

Where The King and the Priest is there GOD is. Thy Bed will flow with pomegranates and scents from dromedary will be yours to find.

Woman you pleasure me. I wouldn't give my wife away.

"I will sleep with a King for life. I will wife a King for Life. I will Bride of Christ for Life. I have slept with a King for love". She has?

Who is a wife?

A wife is the female partner in a Marriage. She is the legitimate female gender in a marriage to a Man. Wife's is spouses, friends, mothers, children, sisters, daughters and could be many more things. There are women of the scripture that were wives they are i.e Sarah, Rebekah, Lea, Rachel, Deborah, Esther, Hannah, Peninah, Elizabeth, Mary and so on.

What is a wife?

A wife is a priceless jewel. Worth more than rubies, she is for honour. She is a beauty. She is a daughter and friend.A wife is a substance. A woman of substance, value, Unique object of speculation. To do the king good all his days.

When to be a wife?

I will say you can be a wife whenever you like. If your heart convicts you. You have someone greater than your conscience and knows all things.

Be a wife when you know you want to be a wife. But ensure you are among them who have prepared themselves. You know your sins will find you out where you have failed. There's no hiding from the king. He knows who you are.

Age wise speaking they say 18 years some say 21 some 25, 26 some 30. I tell you? You know when it is you are required as a wife. Be ready sure you are prepared and make thy home with the King at heart. Let a King and Priest be thy Husband indeed. There be many that have married at middle and old age I think they have a tale to tell with the king and Priest.

Why to be a wife?

You will be a wife because it's required of you. It's the reason for thy existence. It's where the glory is.

How is a Wife?

And GOD did cause Adam to sleep and took from him a rib and formed a woman. For GOD had said it wasn't good for man to be alone, hence he formed the woman: I will make him a help meet.

And Adam agreed and said this indeed is the bone of my bone and flesh of my flesh. She shall be called woman because she was taken out of man.

A wife she shall be by covenant.

A bride is an undefiled woman. Stop this crazy stunt of reckless promiscuous living. When you where thy garments let it flow from a pure heart, from purity. Holiness. Even if you once laid with a man or were raped or molested or whatever. Take up that upheaval task of making thy garments be sparkling white indeed.

Don't throw your pearls to pigs. You are so desperate for marriage and you don't give yourself any value. I tell you they trap women and take them as slaves in the art of a pleasure unapproved. Give thy time to learning, beauty, family, work, do thy business, go out with your peer groups of your own gender and seat at the feet of elderly women and learn. Spend time with Daddy and if you don't have a dad. I tell you GOD is thy father and will take you in.

CHAPTER 3: SEND THY GIFTS FROM AFAR

Diamonds are a woman's best friend. Expensive they are and rear to find. Who will afford such a priced Jewel? Ladies please!

Multitudes of Women Echoing:

"It is for the GREAT KING to BUY AND SEND THEM OUT".

Don't throw your pearls to pigs they did trample on it.

When them priest should call out for a Bride to wife. Abraham did tell you that he sent out his BOX of Jewels from his finest mines for it is fit for a bride. It did get him a wife to Bride his son.

GOD of course was there, He is. Was he that initiated the whole affair.

GOLD MYRR FRANKINCENSE was the perfume for a GREAT KING and you fail to give him the honour.

HE will never share his glory with any man neither will he give his praises to another.

You are for his pleasure. You are well existed and created.

A virtuous woman is hard to find. Her worth is like a priceless ruby. The Alabaster Box woman did tell you her expensive ointment was fit for A King, A great King at that.

I haven't seen why I have to go through this regularly. Ladies smile; there's a Knife to your throat. *You will have to be specially courteous to adhere to the acceptable standard behaviour for being called a wife.*Dont talk back when am talking. Say you're angry at the lowest pitch of your voice. Break your plates when you can no longer tolerate. Scream out your lungs and crouch to the floor wait for him to throw his arms if he really loved you. Some will just stare coldly or sternly and say woman clean this mess up. There they storm out. I did never leave my mama for marriage if I could go to school regularly from the house and catch a late night movie with popcorn then crouch to my bed and sleep.

When you serve a king he did nourish you. Speaking of them kings who have GOD and Christ the Great King as their head. It is a leading to ensure that he loves his wife. Woman will scent of flowers in such an environment.

Tell him you want lovemaking and his readily available giving you a hint his interested. I don't need you to help me do the dishes now just need us to talk tonight. When women pillow talk they know their king did give them a listening ear. Say like spread forth thy sceptre as King Ahaseuarus told Esther you may come in after she inquired of the lord. A king who has himself a wife and Bride will find her do him good all his days. Some say it's a learning to get them brothers' talk with you like that but within the years time may tilt that pillow into your favour. But some never ever find grace in his favour.

Gladly ladies smile. You have yourself a Husband, hence occupy your time: work, read, nurse your children, pray. Never should GOD see that grumpy atmosphere all around you. They say some men rather be served and serviced than serve you at all. I did be sharing some stories about relationships:

Send thy gifts from afar, what did Mother teach you. She said lily wake up, Brush your teeth, have your bath take thy breakfast and get to school, early it must be, keep to thy routine.

Did mother not teach you to carefully make choices? Which is thy favourite subject Maths, English, or Biology? What will you major in Arts, Commerce, or Sciences. Church or not.

To be or not to be.

To hold or not to hold

To love or not to love

For richer or for Poorer

Till death do us apart.

Don't throw your pearls to pigs they did trample on it. Send your gifts from afar for a great king his pedigree, will do you fine all your days. If you lay on the softest mattress Bed imported from Rome and pillows with feathers from Greece, tapestry of Europe and upholstery from London, furniture from Russia and I mustn't forget his holiness. You wouldn't mind you only stay in bed and nursed his children. So "you" Swag that thing. Ladies Smile display your dentition; Your teeth. Tell Mira: Bring my Children to me. Feed me while on the bed. Let's lead our children by the shepherds' gate. Lie down close to the beach and watch the sun set. Thereon retire to bed before your grace arrives. You know; he did attend to you if his Kingship had his holiness "A priest" Crested to it. *Mother am home, "Plant your kisses, how was your day! I am a little bit famished.* You did be glad that he planted a kiss on your 'head'

You wouldn't be strangled I tell you. *He would give you a cold stare where you abandon him in his heart, he will beg you with a straight face and will do his part and say "after you".*

I wonder how them women cope.

To submit by love or to submit by force the pendulum is in your hands. Carefully ladies, wisely make your choice. The alabaster box woman will tell you she knew them men, her ointment was at a high price. Hence she damned the consequences and poured it at he's feet.

I wonder why: *I did rather cover my body, let my skirts go down to my ankle; add a veil to hide my head. Cover my nose and mouth where it was(is) necessary.*

She never gives her bride away that easily, I did never give my wife away; I have slept with the king for love. I will Bride and Wife for life.

Carefully Ladies: Learn a Handwork.

Carefully Ladies: Learn your chores.

Carefully ladies: Read your Books at School.

Carefully Ladies: Say your prayers of forgiveness.

Never forget to chip in for the fruits of the spirit.

It did do you good all your days.

There are Gifts for a Bride and Wife. '

''Kpukoo, Cukoo, Cukoo''.

Gifts for a charming woman.

A king and a priest will need to see that his woman is knowledgeable and well skilled. It doesn't mean that she must go work elsewhere but there are things he did like to see you channel this things to that you are and you have toward. Even if you are a home maker. You learnt how to bake. Bake for the children, for your husband, for relatives and close family Friends. You know how to sew. Sew the bed sheets and curtains for the house the children your room and take some to your pastor too. You educated use it in his enterprise to work for him or with him. Tell him that you could help with the family business or job. Use the career and do something innovative around the house. Like draw up spending Memos, Keep Diaries, Draw up notes on accounts, Draw up feeding time table, monitor lights and water and consumption habits. Show your king and Priest you are one in a million and don't be a sluggard or lazy woman around the house notwithstanding he gave you the leverage. Be awake when he comes back from work. Seat at the Dining table or greet him with hugs in the bed. Marriage is beautiful in all and the bed undefiled but for whoremongers and adulterers GOD will judge.

They will Queen this woman. Her husband is concerned but he has a wife and A Bride in her. His carefully watching after you, he rather preferred that you kept strictly to wife and Bride.

A king will do them good all their days. His carefully prepared for the task he has taken up. He knows how to attend his subjects; glad he will be to see you give him strength all his days. He rather wife you than Queen you. Ask Queen Esther she did tell you she shivered before she approached the king. What? She was a Queen. Every woman must adhere to the acceptable conduct of womanhood in the society. They never Queen their wives. You queen them. You are strictly a queen because you are received by the people: The People approve of you. He never queens his wife.

Queen Vashti will tell you He did never queen his wife. The people agreed with the king and sent her packing. The king was more interested in his honour, preserving his kingdom, his name and his authority inclusive of his royalty. What she had done will cause the women to no longer respect their husbands at home. Personally I would have preferred that King Ahaseuarus simply said *she fell my hands where my highest ranking staffs and guest were. It was egocentric.*

Blessings: He's Kingdom shall know no end

He's will be done on earth as it is in heaven

Glory and Honour he will find.

He will give us this day our daily bread.

"TO HIS COY MISTRESS"
Had we but world enough, and time,
This coyness, lady, were no crime.
We would sit down, and think which way
To walk, and pass our long love's day.
Thou by the Indian Ganges' side
Should'st rubies find: I by the tide
Of Humber would complain, I would
Love you ten years before the flood,
And you should, if you please, refuse
Till the conversion of the Jews.
My vegetable love should grow
Vaster than empires, and more slow ;
An hundred years should go to praise
Thine eyes, and on thy forehead gaze ;
Two hundred to adore each breast,
But thirty thousand to the rest ;
An age at least to every part,
And the last age should show your heart ;
For, lady, you deserve this state,
Nor would I love at lower rate.

But at my back I always hear
Time's winged chariot hurrying near;
And yonder all before us lie
Deserts of vast eternity.
Thy beauty shall no more be found,
Nor, in thy marble vault, shall sound
My echoing song: then worms shall try
That long-preserved virginity,
And you quaint honor turn to dust,

And into ashes all my lust :
The grave's a fine and private place,
But none, I think, do there embrace.
Now, therefore, while the youthful hue
Sits on thy skin like morning dew,
And while thy willing soul transpires
At every pore with instant fires,
Now let us sport us while we may,
And now, like amorous birds of prey,
Rather at once our time devour,
Than languish in his slow-chapt power.
Let us roll all our strength and all
Our sweetness up into one ball,
And tear our pleasures with rough strife
Thorough the iron gates of life :
Thus, though we cannot make our sun
Stand still, yet we will make him run.

By Andrew Marvell (1621-1678).

CHAPTER 4: SUBMISSION

Why Marry?

Because it was GODs original intention for man not to be alone: Gen 2:18.

To avoid Fornication 1 Corinthians 7:2 ,1 Thessalonians 4:3-5

Because the children of this world marry and are given in marriage Luke 20:34

There will be, a Submission in love and there will be, involuntary humility (Submission by Force). Both are used paradoxically. You can use them both interchangeably.

When you seat in thy Labour sits. You will know that this child must come forth. You wouldn't dare return to thy king's chamber without handing him the fruits of his affection. Or should I say fruits of his expectation.

1000 yrs to adore those breasts...

Thy two Breasts are like two young roes that are twins which feed among the lilies.

Hmmn "I wonder why I write so passionately". It is a gift from GOD.

Build thy walls high tower. *For I have a sister she hath no breast ("We have a little sister she has no breast"): what shall we do for our sister in the day when she shall be spoken for? If she be a wall we will build upon her a palace of silver: And if she be a door, we will in close her with boards of cedar.*

Let all know how gracious and good our GOD is.

Grip thy fruit of thy womb with care it is thy possession. Say thy covering and acceptance in he's sight: To love or not to love, to hold or not to hold, for richer or for Poorer. Till death do you part.

What is Submission?

The action of accepting or yielding to a superior force or to the will or authority of another person.

Why is Submission?

The whole duty of man is to fear GOD and keep his command-ment. Ecclesiastes 12:13, because man (speaking of both gender) is created to be served or to serve.

Who is Submission?

Submission is you and me. Learning to submit to one another in love. Learning to worship GOD for who he is and his love.

When is Submission?

Submission is now and forever. It's for the life on earth and the afterlife to come.

How is Submission?

Submission is possible when you agree. Better preferred than when forced or impeded on you. It is humility. Lowliness of mind. Meekness.

I tell you, you won't like were GOD to insist on you submission to a man that does not respond to your love language or appeal to you but in GODs submission you will learn and gain Life. You shall come to know Joy from it. It's preferable that submission be from love. Better to get it right the first time. Carefully make your choices women. Submit to one another in love is an instruction from the Holy Ghost.

Let me explain some things on submission from Esther

1 Now it came to pass in the days of Ahasuerus, (this is Ahasuerus which reigned, from India even unto Ethiopia, over an hundred and seven and twenty provinces:)

2 That in those days, when the king Ahasuerus sat on the throne of his kingdom, which was in Shushan the palace,

3 In the third year of his reign, he made a feast unto all his princes and his servants; the power of Persia and Media, the nobles and princes of the provinces, being before him:

4 When he shewed the riches of his glorious kingdom and the honour of his excellent majesty many days, even an hundred and fourscore days.

5 And when these days were expired, the king made a feast unto all the people that were present in Shushan the palace, both unto great and small, seven days, in the court of the garden of the king's palace;

6 Where were white, green, and blue, hangings, fastened with cords of fine linen and purple to silver rings and pillars of marble: the beds were of gold and silver, upon a pavement of red, and blue, and white, and black, marble.

7 And they gave them drink in vessels of gold, (the vessels being diverse one from another,) and royal wine in abundance, according to the state of the king.

8 And the drinking was according to the law; none did compel: for so the king had appointed to all the officers of his house, that they should do according to every man's pleasure.

9 Also Vashti the queen made a feast for the women in the royal house which belonged to king Ahasuerus.

10 On the seventh day, when the heart of the king was merry with wine, he commanded Mehuman, Biztha, Harbona, Bigtha, and Abagtha, Zethar, and Carcas, the seven chamberlains that served in the presence of Ahasuerus the king,

11 To bring Vashti the queen before the king with the crown royal, to shew the people and the princes her beauty: for she was fair to look on.

12 But the queen Vashti refused to come at the king's commandment by his chamberlains: therefore was the king very wroth, and his anger burned in him.

13 Then the king said to the wise men, which knew the times, (for so was the king's manner toward all that knew law and judgment:

14 And the next unto him was Carshena, Shethar, Admatha, Tarshish, Meres, Marsena, and Memucan, the seven princes of Persia and Media, which saw the king's face, and which sat the first in the kingdom;)

15 What shall we do unto the queen Vashti according to law, because she hath not performed the commandment of the king Ahasuerus by the chamberlains?

16 And Memucan answered before the king and the princes, Vashti the queen hath not done wrong to the king only, but also to all the princes, and to all the people that are in all the provinces of the king Ahasuerus.

¹⁷ For this deed of the queen shall come abroad unto all women, so that they shall despise their husbands in their eyes, when it shall be reported, The king Ahasuerus commanded Vashti the queen to be brought in before him, but she came not.

¹⁸ Likewise shall the ladies of Persia and Media say this day unto all the king's princes, which have heard of the deed of the queen? Thus shall there arise too much contempt and wrath.

¹⁹ If it please the king, let there go a royal commandment from him, and let it be written among the laws of the Persians and the Medes, that it be not altered, That Vashti come no more before king Ahasuerus; and let the king give her royal estate unto another that is better than she.

²⁰ And when the king's decree which he shall make shall be published throughout all his empire, (for it is great,) all the wives shall give to their husbands honour, both to great and small.

²¹ And the saying pleased the king and the princes; and the king did according to the word of Memucan:

²² For he sent letters into all the king's provinces, into every province according to the writing thereof, and to every people after their language, that every man should bear rule in his own house, and that it should be published according to the language of every people.

With the kind permission of the court and the Pardon of His Holiness, I seek his grace to further speak; I am of the perspective that the marriage between Queen Esther and King Ahaseuarus is built on two words 'Opportunity' and 'Prejudice'. As I have rightly perceived. I am of this understanding based on a careful synopsis of the downplay of events from verse 1 of this chapter to the end and still going to the first few chapters of chapter 2.

I am of course to relate this to the word of GOD or the law of GOD as it is the bedrock of our Christian faith.

Now verse one from above has made known to us the person of the king his royal majesty.

His fame was such that he was able to invite all his princes and his servants; the power of Persia and Media, the nobles and princes of the provinces, being before him. And when these days were expired, the king made a feast unto all the people that were present in Shushan the palace, both unto great and small, seven days, in the court of the garden of the king's palace.

This depicts the caliber of people present at the feast. There were two feast held.

Verse 6 shows the extent of the riches of the king even speaking on his *appearing* His servants his upholstery and tapestry. Where were white, green, and blue, hangings, fastened with cords of fine linen and purple to silver rings and pillars of marble: the beds were of gold and silver, upon a pavement of red, and blue, and white, and black, marble. And they gave them drink in vessels of gold, (the vessels being diverse one from another,) and royal wine in abundance, according to the state of the king. *The feast lasted for quite a number of days. Many days at that.*

Apart from the fact that the king had his own guest, Queen Vashti likewise attended to the women.

It happened that the king was merry; good it wasn't tipsy because he and the guest drank according to law maybe Vashti would have gotten herself some beating.

On the seventh day, when the heart of the king was merry with wine, he commanded Mehuman, Biztha, Harbona, Bigtha, and Abagtha, Zethar, and Carcas, the seven chamberlains that served in the presence of Ahasuerus the king,

[11] To bring Vashti the queen before the king with the crown royal, to shew the people and the princes her beauty: for she was fair to look on.

[12] But the queen Vashti refused to come at the king's commandment by his chamberlains: therefore was the king very wroth, and his anger burned in him.

Her refusal caused the king to inquire from the men who knew times and eventually she was put away and agreed that another should take her place.

Likewise shall the ladies of Persia and Media say this day unto all the king's princes, which have heard of the deed of the queen? Thus shall there arise too much contempt and wrath.

Take cognizance that her action was said to be possible to cause a negative influence on women and hence a decree was sent out that Men should bare the rule in their house hold.

Chapter 2 verse 1-2 says when the king remembered her Vashti's action he asked that virgins should be brought to him to make choice for remarriage.

My Ruling: I am personally of the view that this two should be arrested and confined to a room alone warm so that they can both talk to themselves. Honestly what was Vashti thinking his such an honourable man. She did injure the ego of her king and really I feel the pain of feeling neglected and unappreciated or disrespected but I wish somehow the king would have made a way out for Vashti. Maybe Vashti didn't get the opportunity to apologize in person to him. Maybe she has been exhibiting strange attitudes which the king could no longer tolerate and that day was just his opportunity out. But I tell you women are of such persuasive influence in the homes. I wish somehow royal letters were sent out with kings signet and under Queen Vashti's handwriting her signature and Kings signature as well; giving an apology over her behavior at the feast to all the invitees because personally I think Vashti was a beautiful and well sophisticated woman moreover she's the first wife only that GODs plan must not fail in humanity.

I tell you there are some queens that will get that "Apology" on their behalf, but let's just say it was the will of GOD. Because I tell you the Yahweh that I know does not approve of the showing of oneself or everything he has to people. That I learnt in the story of Hezekiah which I earlier adumbrated as found in 2nd Kings 20:13-18.

...^{13} And Hezekiah hearkened unto them and shewed them all the house of his precious things, the silver, and the gold, and the spices, and the precious ointment, and all the house of his armour, and all that was found in his treasures: there was nothing in his house, nor in all his dominion, that Hezekiah shewed them not.

^{14} Then came Isaiah the prophet unto king Hezekiah, and said unto him, What said these men? and from whence came they unto thee? And Hezekiah said, They are come from a far country, even from Babylon.

¹⁵ And he said, What have they seen in thine house? And Hezekiah answered, All the things that are in mine house have they seen: there is nothing among my treasures that I have not shewed them.

¹⁶ And Isaiah said unto Hezekiah, Hear the word of the Lord.

¹⁷ Behold, the days come, that all that is in thine house, and that which thy fathers have laid up in store unto this day, shall be carried into Babylon: nothing shall be left, saith the Lord.

¹⁸ And of thy sons that shall issue from thee, which thou shalt beget, shall they take away; and they shall be eunuchs in the palace of the king of Babylon.

The showing of one's excellent majesty is frowned at by GOD. Nebuchadnezzar failed to return glory to GOD at some point and lost his wits and became like an animal.

When he "King Ahaseuarus" shewed the riches of his glorious kingdom and the honour of his excellent majesty many days, even an hundred and fourscore days.

Personally I feel that what transpired was done by GOD to help preserve the kings Kingship and kingdom. GOD had seen this coming that he the king may possibly loose his kingdom because this was the case with Hezekiah remember GODs words...

YOU DON'T SHOW ALL YOUR EXCELLENT MAJESTY TO PEOPLE THAT ARE STRANGERS TO YOUR LAND ITS NEVER DONE. Nebuchadnezzar is another example. It was for opportunity and Prejudice. And the Jews were GODs people they had pleased GOD somehow and were used and Preserved by mercy and covenant.

Let's put our hands together for GOD who can't cease to be GOD to everyone. So great is his mercy he does wonders hallelujah.

On Vashti am very passionate over her because I don't think that because she was put away does mean she's a bad wife or has always put up that attitude. Personally it could be that she was ill that day or the way of a woman was on her or that she was in the heat of gist with fellow women and thus couldn't oblige to her king. I think that women we actually need to be on our knees or on the alert because submission entails that we be prepared for it when it is required from us. Because I can tell you favor is needed at some point in time where husbands are and that Queen Vashti lacked that favor, that day and period. Some other woman may have done this and been covered up by the king and forgiven. Even covered up where people are. Queen Vashti didn't see this coming. But thank GOD that he comforts people.

Will you be in submission by Love or by compulsion? Will it be by willingness of heart or by force? You decide. Carefully make your choice in marriage. It will be preferred to wed a King and Priest. I tell you a Priest is necessary to add to your king. You don't want to put up with the kings anger without his priesthood.

CHAPTER 5: A PRICELESS JEWEL... (DIRTY/ DEEP SECRETE)

Adam, Adam I wasn't the one that asked you to eat of that fruit you ate it on your own volition. Nevertheless the woman shall be delivered in child bearing. If she continues in faith and charity and holiness with sobriety. First Timothy 2:15

Will they say you are the one that made them or they will not. For behind every successful man is a woman.

What my son/ and what, the son of my womb/ and what, the son of my vows? Give not thy strength unto women, nor thy ways to that which destroyed kings.

It is not for kings, O lemuel; it is not for kings to drink wine; nor for princes strong drink:

Lest they drink and forget the law,

And pervert the judgement of any of the afflicted. Give a strong drink unto him that is ready to perish, and wine unto those that be of heavy hearts.

Let him drink and forget his poverty, and remember his misery no more...

Who can find a virtuous woman?

A King and A priest its he's to get a Virtuous woman. For we are a chosen generation, royal priesthood, an holy nation, a peculiar People; that ye should shew forth the praises of him who hath called you out of darkness to his marvellous light: which in time past were not a people, but are now the people of GOD: which had not obtained mercy, but now have obtained mercy.

10 Who can find a virtuous woman? for her price is far above rubies.

11 The he art of her husband doth safely trust in her, so that he shall have no need of spoil.

12 She will do him good and not evil all the days of her life.

13 She seeketh wool, and flax, and worketh willingly with her hands.

14 She is like the merchants' ships; she bringeth her food from afar.

15 She riseth also while it is yet night, and giveth meat to her household, and a portion to her maidens.

16 She considereth a field, and buyeth it: with the fruit of her hands she planteth a vineyard.

17 She girdeth her loins with strength, and strengtheneth her arms.

18 She perceiveth that her merchandise is good: her candle goeth not out by night.

19 She layeth her hands to the spindle, and her hands hold the distaff.

20 She stretcheth out her hand to the poor; yea, she reacheth forth her hands to the needy.

21 She is not afraid of the snow for her household: for all her household are clothed with scarlet.

22 She maketh herself coverings of tapestry; her clothing is silk and

purple.

23 Her husband is known in the gates, when he sitteth among the elders

of the land.

24 She maketh fine linen, and selleth it; and delivereth girdles unto the

merchant.

25 Strength and honour are her clothing; and she shall rejoice in time to

come.

26 She openeth her mouth with wisdom; and in her tongue is the law of

kindness.

27 She looketh well to the ways of her household, and eateth not the

bread of idleness.

28 Her children arise up, and call her blessed; her husband also, and he

praiseth her.

29 Many daughters have done virtuously, but thou excellent them all.

30 Favour is deceitful, and beauty is vain: but a woman that feareth the

Lord, she shall be praised.

31 Give her of the fruit of her hands; and let her own works praise her in the gates.

He doesn't ever agree shes good, he knows exactly what his doing. It's a Deep secret. He will say you are nothing. It's a dirty secret. He will let you be, let the earth know that you are virtue itself. He will never ever hide you from his people. He will let every eye know that you are a Virtuous woman.

For the Deep secret he doesn't want to loose you even if its at your expense, He will keep you to himself and hide your value or beauty. He will want to be the one only seen and I tell you that ego and jealousy may be roleplayed here not just love. For the Dirty secret. He may be weak in an area and you are able to cover those weaknesses, you may be his soul mate his heart trust in you and he sees nothing in your being known. His family loves you and everyone loves you and he can't hide his joy over you. You are befitting for a wife hence the agree that you be. His watching you, I tell you, one slight blunder you could lose it all, everything could crumble down. Just carefully make your choices in marriage ladies. Study temperaments and love languages and ensure while you court you notice he's a King and Priest. Stay away from non royalties, when they royal become kings before priest, they want to dump you. They don't know your value or worth. But if they attain priesthood before Kingship they know the value of you as their wife. But if they are both at a time. Then you are lucky. Lady you could swag that thing. You got yourself a "Husband".

To be or not to be; please wed a King it doesn't matter whether deep or Dirty, you still have yourself your ointment, oil and flax.

Exodus 21:9-10

And if he have betrothed her unto his son, he shall deal with her after the manner of daughters.

[10] If he takes him another wife; her food, her raiment, and her duty of marriage, shall he not diminish?

CHAPTER 6: DESTITUTE OR DEPENDENT OR THY OWN BOSSES MAN.

To win or not to win. To conquer or not to conquer. To rule or not to rule. Thy time and chance will come. GOD is; he will. Let thy head be bowed in contrition let thy feet not feeble be. Let thy head be bowed in prayer. Let thy mouth never go short of his word.

Woman you can't leave like one infirmed all your life, you can't be a burden to a man or a liability. You must arise. Get up all things are ready. Look around you everything has fallen in your pleasant places. The woman bowed down by the issue of Blood knew exactly what healing did for her. A dependent woman can pass as good where she depends by the word but are you specially prepared to take up that task. That responsibility. It means you live on the sole bread winner/Sole Provider. But some of our women can't appreciate this. We are not groomed for this line of marriage. Hence we bite in marriage, complain, murmur and grumble. That your husband is the sole bread winner in marriage and is wealthy does not mean that if his travelling to a foreign country he must go with you. It's a call to serve. You will have to die to yourself. If you are your own bosses man good for you. You know you have to carefully iron this out before the marriage. If you have to sign agreements before marriage to this effect it is good, if you have to involve the important necessary party or parties in this it's good. You have to be humble about this. You have to know your man and insist you be your own boss. We women can do all things but we have to apply discretion and wisdom to it. Dont be without yourself when getting yourself into marriage.

Do you know that many life's have been lost, Destinies have been truncated and Purposes unfulfilled because of the wrong perception to marriage or not properly laying your bed before lying on it. When it comes to child bearing that Ada is able to multitask in childbearing, with her job and marriage does not mean that Abimbola can do so. Some women are fragile and can't cope once they start childbearing. They need helpers around, need house maids or nanies, family relatives like mother or sisters or cousins living with them to help in the early part of the child bearing and child growth or growing up. Some need a very conducive environment to turn out well or bring out the best in them as mothers and wives. Some need the love and reception of their husbands to flourish in the marriage.Where the environment is not conducive how will you learn? Poor health environment may not work for you. Poor feeding, Poor hygiene, Poor Health care or condition may destroy you as a mother and wife. Hence ensure you wed a King and a Priest.

What about Temperaments (Why you act the way you do)? By Tim lahaye

Sanguines, Melancholy, Phlegmatics, Cholerics. More often two Tempraments mix or three. But one is often more dominant. You need to understand your spouses temperament. It will help in marriage. I learnt opposites attract. I recommend buying the book it's written by Tim Lahaye

Languages of Love? Gary Chapman (Buy the book and read) says there are five languages of love namely: Acts of service, Physical Touch, Words of affirmation, Receiving Gifts, Quality time. Your man must understand your love language and you his also. It helps keep the marriage growing where its a give and take.

It's a whole lot of things. It takes the presence of the Holy Ghost to make you outstanding or go with you all the way to help you through your marriage and more often than not where you took the wrong partner it is you that the Holy Ghost will groom or work on before he faces your spouse. Rarely will he face that spouse unless he is satisfied with your change or changed heart. So why take the risk. Like late Bimbo Odukoya will say: "Marry" your friend. I tell you GOD Christ is a Great King and High Priest. Hence if you wed a king and Priest it means you wed a son of GOD. Don't separate the Priest from the King. The two must go hand in hand.

The Bosses Man is in control because she has let GOD be her Lord and GOD. She invited him into her marriage. She is the priceless jewel described in Proverbs 31. She's able to multitask. She has everything working for her good. Everything is going on in her marriage as planned. She has been groomed and trained by GOD and now she has been favoured in her marriage.

Choose this day whom you will serve GOD or Man.

You better choose him; We are not the same people. Your case is not my case. Me I have crucified my flesh.

CHAPTER 7: BROKEN HEARTED OR/AND CRUSHED IN SPIRIT.

You could be broken hearted or crushed in spirit. When your spouse is not responding to you especially for the female folks and you are in love with him. What do you do?

Some take the matter into their hands and begin to argue or quarrel over it. Some withdraw and stay away and never solve the problem. Some engage in denying rights for being unresponded to like sex rights. Some go complain to friends or family. While some may go to the church and complain and undergo counselling.

I advise you to stop and think first. I never like to make decisions hastily especially when vulnerable. This one of the things I learnt in my Christian faith and walk with GOD. Ask yourself salient questions: *1.What really is the problem we are having? 2. What is the Issue on ground? 3. My Spouse is he a King and a Priest or just a King without Priest or yet to uncover the kingship in him and yet his a Priest? 4. Am I at Fault? 5. Have we ever addressed this Problem before? 6. How can we solve this problem?*

Remember to pray over the situation.

The Broken hearted individual is in contrition, his in realisation of his sinful state and in need of GODs healing power. His looking at himself as not being able to that he needs a helping hand to see him through.

The Crushed in spirit is forlorn, He can't, his helpless so needy and pours out his heart in repentance to GOD. Such A person needs comforting by the Holy Ghost. Women may need to come to this stage in their marriage when they are just relinquishing every-thing to GOD because they have tried their best to make that marriage work and it appears that the situation is hopeless hence they are crying out to GOD for Hosanna that he redeems them. They can't by their strength again.

Example:

Suzanne is a woman whose husband is a drunkard and she wasn't lucky to marry him as a king and Priest. They are both of the middle class. Average. Suzanne needs a friend in him but can't get that because of his drinking habits. She explores talking to family about his weakness, she undergoes counselling with him and even he goes for rehabilitation and his out to pick it up again. Suzanne is going to need to cry out to GOD Hosanna for her partner because she just can't again. The nights he come back 12am, The times she gets battered by him physically, the times her neighbours knock at her door to tell her that her husband slept at their frontage. Their failed finances. She's just crushed in spirit and has to ask GOD to redeem her husband and make him a priest again and king him for her.

Really I don't advise people to go the way of being unsure of their spouse or marriage partner. Marry A King and A Priest. He's a friend. Jesus is A Great King and A High Priest hence marry by the Lord. A King and Priest is a Son of GOD. 1 Peter 2:9 calls us a Chosen generation, A Royal Priesthood... what are you waiting for. The Bulk of responsibility attached for not wedding a Royal Priesthood may be too much for you to bear. You may not even be able to survive or cope in that situation. Why put GOD to the test. I tell you as I earlier shared. More often than not where it is the woman that defaults in making the right decision of a marriage partner she may be the one in marriage that will have to endure and GOD may come to change only her and prepare her for the marriage the way it is to deal with it and emerge strong. Hardly or scarcely or should I use seldom will GOD also work on the Male partner or change. He only does that on rare occasions.

You can choose to be cast down all your life and refuse to dream again or fulfil your life plan or expectation or you can rise up and forgive and move on with your life. Go dream big, do the things that make you happy,, go live life.

Please women you are a Priceless Gem. Don't throw your pearls to pigs they will trample on it. Diamonds are a woman's best friend. Be sincere and GOD will establish and bless you. He will keep you in perfect peace.

CHAPTER 8: FINAL WORDS OF PARTING. RESIGN TO FAITH.

What will you like to hear? Dump your man when he doesn't meet your expectation? You won't be hearing that through my lips.

However I can't see why people in marriage can't get the best out of it. if they only key into the prophetic. There are scriptures from the bible that tell you GODs mind towards man in respect to marriage and towards you in respect to your marriage. Institute the word over your situation.

Faith says substance of things hoped belief in things not yet seen. By it the elders obtained a good report.

You can have a good report if you do your part. Don't give up just yet. There are deliverance services you can undergo at various bible believing churches. Which I know will liberate you from problems in your marriage.

You can locate 'me' Author of this book and I will put you through.

Faith says ability in incapacity; it says not your own kind of faith but the word kind of faith.

Men ought to pray and not to faint. Keep praying about your life partner, your children, your plans, destiny and purpose. Don't give up just yet.

So I tell you ladies what to do when Honey starts misbehaving, especially for them that have children, Take a hot tea and start working, improvise instructional materials as teaching aids and manoeuvre teaching methods. Smile at him always; ask him will he be eating breakfast or dinner, wear your best lingerie, put on the most appealing night wears. Pay him unexpected visits at the office and don't go empty handed. Either send a message or email to him or take a gift to him or drive down during lunch hours and take a meal to him or take your meals with him. If you close from work before him or at the same time, drive to the office and wait to come home with him. Smile to your husband. Don't burden him with responsibilities you already have yourself a job. Treat him like a boy again or a newly wedded spouse. Ask him questions says Holy Ghost. 'He' questions. Why my love is…, what my love is…, how do we…, who is…, when do you…

Ask me 'He' questions says Holy Ghost? His banner over me is love.

And for them women whose husbands are sole providers what will I be doing for you. You would have to be extra courteous or submissive. How did you let this go so far, how did you let things get so bad. Grab your man hard and tell him you can't do without him. That you built your whole life around him. Let your tears run down your eyes like a tap and save that marriage it's your reward. Crouch to the floor and put your heads at his feet and let your tears drip on his toes, go to his ties and rest your head and say to him my lord, I can't live without you I am an empty woman without your love. Please stay with me in this marriage. We did make things work. I will be a better person a better woman for you. I can. And for them that run businesses and estates and have jobs or work try this and your husband did stun you did this for him. It's a romantic gesture to keep the fire of your marriage burning.

Don't give it all away. Unless you married a monster or beast but I tell you some beast could turn to a charming prince. Go ask Beauty she did tell you the story of Beauty and the beast.

Prayer: Father I will not be unfortunate in life. I will not be unopportuned in life. Father I refuse to be disfavoured in life. In Yeshua Ha-

mashiach name Amen.

CONCLUSION

I don't know what your expectations are about marriage but I have my. The days we were virgins we didn't know much about this things but we concerned ourselves with the lord but after marriage we developed to womanhood and are still virgins at heart for being virgins in marriage but we did tell you that your expectation should not be cut short. What do you want from marriage? Did you prepare? I tell you presently am not with my spouse but it took me a lot of pain to still keep being Christian and keep the faith. It's quite a surprise that GOD should satisfy me with a writing ministry because I never thought I will be a writer before I had married my ex.

Your value is above rubies. You can't let anyone who does not see this worth ruin you. You must carefully make good choices as to marriage. Wed yourself a KING and A PRIEST. Think about those that are looking up to you, the heart break you did cause if your marriage is not going as expected or planned, The health challenges you may incur for being abandoned or alone, The wrong impression you may create where you can't wriggle out of the mess and make the best out of your life. The years of bitterness and unforgiveness you may be forced to live in.

This book offers so much to the reader on marriage. It's a whole lot in its entirety. Marry the right man. Marry a GODly Partner. Marry your king and Priest. Christ is the head of such a husband. He likewise will do you good all your days.

CHANT!

Who will sleep with a King for life?

I will!

Who will wife the King for Life?

I will!

Who will Bride of Christ for Life?

I will!

I have slept with a king for love before

She has?

Music:

She will Sleep with a king for Life.(2ce)

Who will sleep with a king for Life.

You are absolutely crazy.(low key)

Well we think so.(two (2) guys speak)

All the same (at the top of her voice)

I will sleep with a king for Life.

Tananananananana Tanana